Oops!

ALL ABOUT OPPOSITES

Written by Kirsten Hall

Illustrated by Bev Luedecke

children's press®

A Division of Scholastic Inc.
New York   Toronto   London   Auckland   Sydney
Mexico City   New Delhi   Hong Kong
Danbury, Connecticut

About the Author

Kirsten Hall, formerly an early-childhood teacher,
is a children's book editor in New York City. She has been
writing books for children since she was thirteen years old
and now has over sixty titles in print.

About the Illustrator

Bev Luedecke enjoys life and nature in Colorado.
Her sparkling personality and artistic flair are reflected in her
creation of Beastieville, a world filled with lovable Beasties
that are sure to delight children of all ages.

Library of Congress Cataloging-in-Publication Data

Hall, Kirsten.
  Oops! : all about opposites / written by Kirsten Hall ; illustrated by
Bev Luedecke.
      p. cm.
Summary: Zip and Pip race up and down, high and low, always wanting to
go fast, not its opposite, slow.
  ISBN 0-516-22895-1 (lib. bdg.)   0-516-24657-7 (pbk.)
  [1. English language–Synonyms and antonyms. 2. Stories in rhyme.] I.
Luedecke, Bev, ill. II. Title.
  PZ8.3.H146Oo 2003
  428.1–dc21

                              2003001582

1 2 3 4 5 6 7 8 9 10 R 12 11 10 09 08 07 06 05 04 03

A NOTE TO PARENTS AND TEACHERS

Welcome to the world of the Beasties, where learning is FUN. In each of the charming stories in this series, the Beasties deal with character traits that every child can identify with. Each story reinforces appropriate concept skills for kindergartners and first graders, while simultaneously encouraging problem-solving skills. Following are just a few of the ways that you can help children get the most from this delightful series.

Stories to be read and enjoyed

Encourage children to read the stories aloud. The rhyming verses make them fun to read. Then ask them to think about alternate solutions to some of the problems that the Beasties have faced or to imagine alternative endings. Invite children to think about what they would have done if they were in the story and to recall similar things that have happened to them.

Activities reinforce the learning experience

The activities at the end of the books offer a way for children to put their new skills to work. They complement the story and are designed to help children develop specific skills and build confidence. Use these activities to reinforce skills. But don't stop there. Encourage children to find ways to build on these skills during the course of the day.

Learning opportunities are everywhere

Use this book as a starting point for talking about how we use reading skills or math or social studies concepts in everyday life. When we search for a phone number in the telephone book and scan names in alphabetical order or check a list, we are using reading skills. When we keep score at a baseball game or divide a class into even-numbered teams, we are using math.

The more you can help children see that the skills they are learning in school really do have a place in everyday life, the more they will think of learning as something that is part of their lives, not as a chore to be borne. Plus you will be sending the important message that learning is fun.

Madeline Boskey Olsen, Ph.D.
Developmental Psychologist

Bee-Bop

Puddles

Slider

Wilbur

Pip & Zip

Flippet

Pooky

Mr. Rigby

We're the Beasties

Smudge

Toggles

Zip and Pip just love to race.
They race everywhere they go.

"Look at me! I am so fast!
I am fast and you are slow!"

Zip and Pip race by the lake.
"Did you see how fast I went?"

Pip is calling out to Zip.
Oops! She did not see that tent!

"Oh, I did not see you there!
I can fix it! Let me try!"

Wilbur does not want her help.
"I can fix it, Pip. Good-bye!"

Zip and Pip are off again.
Pip calls, "Zip, look! Watch me go!"

Pip is looking back at Zip.
"Look out, Zip! Look out! Oh, no!"

Oops! Zip did not look in time.
He runs right into a tree.

Toggles is down on the ground.
"Slow down, Zip! You might hurt me!"

"Zip and Pip! You must slow down!"
Zip and Pip both nod. "We know!"

"Now I need to pick these up!"
Toggles frowns and off they go.

"Look up there! I see a hill!
That hill looks like so much fun!"

Smudge looks up and then back down.
He has berries in his hair!

"Zip and Pip! You must slow down!"
Smudge is sad. He liked his pie.

"We are sorry," they tell Smudge.
"We are sorry. We will try."

"Zip, I guess we must slow down."
"Pip, that sounds like a good plan."

"Our friends really want us to.
We must show them that we can!"

That night, all the Beasties eat.
"Here come Zip and Pip! Oh, no!"

"There is no need to worry, friends!
From now on, we will go slow!"

COUNTING TIME

1. How many trees have Zip and Pip passed?

2. How many birds are looking at Zip and Pip?

3. Do you remember how many times Zip and Pip run into things?

SOUNDS LIKE...

"Grow" is a word that sounds like "slow." Can you think of any other words that sound like "slow"?

LET'S TALK ABOUT IT

Zip and Pip love racing around town.
But their friends do not want them to.

1. Why do you think their friends
   asked them to slow down?

2. What kinds of things can happen
   when you are moving too fast?

3. Why is it better to move slowly
   sometimes?

4. Do you think Zip and Pip's friends
   will be happy now that they have
   slowed down?

WORD LIST

a	from	know	pick	then
again	frowns	lake	pie	there
all	fun	let	Pip	these
am	go	like	plan	they
and	good	liked	race	this
are	good-bye	look	really	time
at	great	looking	right	to
back	ground	looks	roll	Toggles
Beasties	guess	love	rolls	top
berries	hair	me	run	tree
both	has	might	runs	try
by	he	much	sad	up
calling	help	must	see	us
calls	her	need	she	want
can	here	night	show	watch
come	hill	no	slow	we
could	his	nod	Smudge	went
did	how	not	so	whee
does	hurt	now	sorry	when
down	I	off	sounds	why
eat	in	oh	tell	Wilbur
everywhere	into	on	tent	will
fast	is	oops	that	worry
fix	it	our	the	you
friends	just	out	them	Zip

I just saw you there with Toggles.
Am I seeing things? Oh, dear!"

"Flippet! How could you be swimming?
I just saw you over there!

You were sitting next to Pooky.
You were in a big blue chair!"

"Zip and Pip! How could it be?
How could you be running by?

Are there two of everyone?
What is going on? Oh, my!"

"Come here, everyone!" calls Slider.
"There is something we must do.

You must come with me to see this!
There are two of each of you!"

Toggles meets her friends outside.
"You like my art? I hoped you would!"

Slider opens his eyes wide.
"Toggles, you are really good!"

COLOR COUNT

1. How many of the Beasties have red fur?

2. How many of the Beasties have blue fur?

3. How many of the Beasties have yellow fur?

SOUNDS LIKE...

"Tight" sounds alot like the word "white". What other words do you know that sound like the word "white"?

LET'S TALK ABOUT IT

Slider is surprised to see all of his friends at Toggles' house.

1. How do you think he feels when he sees them all there?

2. How would you feel if all of your friends got together and you did not know?

3. How can you make sure your friends do not ever feel left out?

WORD LIST

a	fun	more	Puddles	there
all	fur	Mr.	rain	things
am	going	much	raining	thinks
and	good	must	reach	this
are	gray	my	really	tie
around	great	myself	red	to
art	green	needs	Rigby	Toggles
away	has	next	room	told
be	he	nice	running	too
big	her	no	sadly	two
blue	here	not	saw	up
brushes	high	now	see	wait
by	his	of	seeing	was
calls	hoped	oh	sees	we
cannot	how	on	she	were
chair	I	one	sitting	wet
come	in	opens	Slider	what
could	is	out	slides	while
dear	it	outside	Smudge	why
do	jars	over	so	wide
does	just	paint	something	will
doing	know	painting	starts	window
done	let	paints	stopped	with
dry	like	passes	sun	would
each	likes	perfect	swimming	yellow
everyone	looks	picture	tall	you
eyes	me	Pip	that	Zip
Flippet	meets	play	the	
friends	mix	Pooky	then	